4

Some Days I Breathe On Purpose

Learning To Be A Calm, Cool Kid

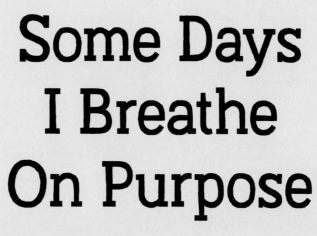

Kellie Doyle Bailey, MA CCC-SLP, MMT/SELI

Illustrated by Hannah Bailey

Some Days I Breathe On Purpose

Published by:
PESI Publishing
3839 White Ave.
Eau Claire, WI 54703

Illustrations: Hannah Bailey
Cover: Hannah Bailey
Layout: Amy Rubenzer

ISBN: 9781683734413

Printed in Canada

PESI Publishing
pesipublishing.com

Hi, I'm Maysie,

and I'm a calm, cool kid.

Flipping my lid means I lose my cool.

It can happen at home, in the car, or at school.

I have two friends—Grace and Max.

They know lots of ways to be calm and relaxed.

Max taught me a new way to learn how to breathe
so I won't flip my lid and fight, run, or freeze.

These new ways are called **MINDFUL TOOLS.**

When we do them **ON PURPOSE** we can be calm and cool.

Here's the truth:
We all flip our lids.
But mindful tools can help
grown-ups and kids.

Would you like these mindful tools?

So you can **CHOOSE ON PURPOSE** to be calm and cool?

Keep on reading and you will see how easy mindful tools can be.

Every day I **REMEMBER TO BREATHE**

when I'm calm and cool or I'm weak in my knees.

Maybe this is silly to you,
because everyone breathes—
it's just what we do.
But breathing on purpose is different, you see,
because... you **BREATHE INTENTIONALLY.**

If you are curious to learn a new way to **BREATHE ON PURPOSE**, night or day, keep turning the pages and I'll show you... everything you need to do.

I BREATHE ON PURPOSE

when I start my day.

I BREATHE ON PURPOSE

when I look both ways.

I BREATHE ON PURPOSE

when I take a walk.

I BREATHE ON PURPOSE
when I feel worry or fear.

I BREATHE ON PURPOSE

when I'm sad or alone.

I BREATHE ON PURPOSE

when I try something new.

I BREATHE ON PURPOSE

when I'm sick with the flu.

I BREATHE ON PURPOSE

when I meet a new friend.

BREATHING ON PURPOSE is simple and neat.
It's a way to calm down from my head to my feet.

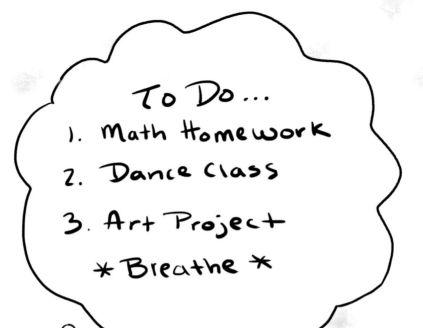

When my mind starts to wander with a memory or plan,

I put my hand on my heart while I sit still or stand.

I breathe a full breath right through my nose.

I soften my eyes and let them stay closed.

My heart stops pounding, and my mind gets a rest.

I go on with my day, just doing my best.

Would you like to try it too?

Before **YOU** flip your lid, before **YOU** lose your cool?

Remember, only you get to choose. The choice is yours—there's nothing to lose.

So the next time you start flipping your lid,

BREATHE ON PURPOSE and be a calm, cool kid.

Teach **BREATHING ON PURPOSE** to your family and friends

so everyone learns to make lid flipping end.

Anyone can be a calm, cool kid.

Anyone can stop flipping their lid.

Anyone can learn mindful ways

to stay calm and cool, night and day.

Now this part's important—please listen to me.

When we **BREATHE ON PURPOSE**, mindfully, then the world is filled with grown-ups and kids just doing our best without flipping our lids. Then everyone is safe at home or school because breathing on purpose keeps us **ALL** calm and cool.

WOULD YOU LIKE TO TRY IT TOO?

Helping children of all ages learn how to **BREATHE ON PURPOSE** is the first practice of mindfulness. Because of the busyness of our days, most of us spend more time doing rather than being. Mind-wandering happens with little awareness on our parts. Practicing mindfulness helps all human beings pay attention to the present moment. When we **BREATHE ON PURPOSE**, we are helping our body, heart, and mind take a well-deserved rest and tap into our first life gift: the breath.

Here's How You Do Mindful Breathing On Purpose

★ Invite your children to practice a mindful body position—noticing any tension in the head, neck, shoulders, torso, and legs, and allow a softening to any area that may be holding onto resistance. It's okay if the tension doesn't go away. Simply noticing and accepting is enough.

★ Keep the belly and chest relaxed and breathe on purpose—in through the nose and out through the mouth. Aim at first for 3 slow deep breaths each time you practice. Remind children that this is a time to pay attention on purpose to their breathing. Eyes can be softly lidded or shut if children feel safe closing their eyes.

★ If you notice that the mind starts to wander during the mindful breathing moment, you can teach your children to anchor their thoughts, memories, or plans by simply stating, "Breathing," "Here," or "Calm." The anchoring word is not as important as noticing that the mind is wandering and returning to present-moment awareness.

Once children have mastered the art of breathing on purpose, try introducing the following **Mindful Breathing Games:**

Counting Breaths: This mindful breathing practice helps children and adults who struggle with being present while breathing on purpose because of the busy mind. Invite your children to count 1, 2, 3 on the in-breath and 4, 5, 6 on the out-breath.

Belly Breathing: This mindful breathing practice is especially fun for preschool-aged children. Invite your children to lay down flat on the floor, place a "Breathing Buddy" (bean bag or small stuffed animal) on each child's stomach, and invite them to take slow deep breaths, paying attention to the Breathing Buddy rising up on the in-breath and lowering down on the out-breath.

3-5 Breathing: This mindful breathing practice is fun for all ages and especially useful in helping everyone feel calm and cool. Begin in a mindful breathing posture and inhale for 3 seconds and exhale for 5 seconds. When we purposefully elongate our exhalation, we stimulate the parasympathetic nervous system (the calming part of our autonomic nervous system).

Energized Balloon Breathing: This mindful breathing practice helps to give everyone a boost of energy during those low and slow moments. This practice is especially helpful after lunch and recess and is great for children of all ages and grade levels. Invite your children to inhale on purpose 5 quick breaths (Breath 1, Breath 2, Breath 3, Breath 4, Breath 5) and exhale long and slow until the lungs deflate like a balloon.

Aim for 3 repetitions of any of these Mindful Breathing On Purpose practices and work up to 5 depending upon your child's attention, motivation, and enjoyment.

NOTE TO FAMILIES, CAREGIVERS & EDUCATORS

Thank you for choosing *Some Days I Breathe on Purpose* and for your interest in exploring mindfulness practices with your children and students. Mindfulness is best explained as taking small moments each day to be intentionally present. **Right here, right now, on purpose.**

Mindfulness is backed by the most recent brain and mind science as being an effective tool to help human beings feel centered and grounded, especially during moments of uncertainty and stress.

Being a kid is tricky, and the demands for learning and growing are plentiful and often complex. It's important to remember that each child develops at their own individual pace and will learn optimally when they feel safe, connected, loved, seen, and valued by caring adults. As adults, we can equip youth with the best tools and strategies so that they can navigate the uncertainties of life and grow to be healthy, happy adults themselves. One way we can help kids is to share a **mindful moment.**

Mindfulness is not just for kids. If you're new to mindfulness, we invite you to take the time to purposefully cultivate self-awareness and self-management skills for yourself. When adults are integrated and regulated, we are better equipped to help our children navigate their own emotions, thoughts, and feelings and to co-regulate. Teach your children to recognize the signs of emotions. Remind them that **all** emotions are okay, but it's not helpful to get stuck in any emotion, thought, or feeling that doesn't serve us in any positive or purposeful way.

Spend time throughout your day noticing where your mind takes you. Ask yourself: *Am I thinking? Am I remembering? Am I planning?* If you catch yourself in a mind-wandering moment, take a few slow, deep breaths and bring yourself back to right here, right now, on purpose—and teach your children how to do this too.

Often our stress comes from replaying situations from our past or worrying about what might happen in the future. When we cultivate a present-moment awareness through the simple practice of breathing (returning to our first life gift), then we can shift away from the stressors that mind-wandering can bring and move through our lives with purposeful connection to **now**.

May you and your children be forever well, safe, healthy, and happy as you calm the heart, mind, and body together through breathing on purpose.

Kellie Doyle Bailey

ACKNOWLEDGMENTS

Following the release of **Some Days I Flip My Lid** (October 2019) and the sequel **Some Nights I Flip My Lid** (2020), Hannah and I began to explore how we could continue to share mindfulness practices with our readers. We received countless messages of appreciation from adults across the country for providing mindful tools they could easily use with children of all ages to support mental health and emotional wellness. We know that it takes "a calm brain and body to calm a brain and body." Thank you for recognizing that in order for our children to be grounded and centered, we must commit to doing our own work first. We hope that you all enjoy Maysie's mindfulness story!

Thank you to our dear friends and colleagues, Deqa Dhalac, Habib Nesta Uwizeyimana, and Amelia Lyons, for sharing your lived experiences and informing our work with compassion and open hearts while ensuring fidelity in our representation of Maysie and her family. To my fellow mindfulness colleagues and friends, Sean Wilson Fargo, J. G. Larochette, and Andrew Nance, we are grateful to be on this mindfulness journey with you. Keep shining your beautiful lights and sharing your gifts with the world!

As always, we'd like to give a nod of appreciation and gratitude to Dr. Dan Siegel for his work on lid flipping and the hand-brain model. Thank you for sharing your work with all of us. For more information about Dr. Siegel's work, please visit www.drdansiegel.com.

KELLIE DOYLE BAILEY, MA, CCC-SLP, MMT/SELI, and **HANNAH G. BAILEY**, BA, are a mother-daughter creative team. Together they brought to life *Some Days I Flip My Lid* and its sequel *Some Nights I Flip My Lid*. Both books are loosely framed around Hannah and her brother Doyle as they navigated the complexities of lid flipping brought on by life's big emotions.

Kellie is a veteran speech-language pathologist of more than 30 years and a certified mindfulness/social-emotional learning (SEL) specialist. She is the founder of Calm Cool Kids Educate™ and provides workshops and trainings for families, educators, and community partners to learn the importance of using mindful practices as a tool for SEL development.

Hannah is a middle school art educator and is pursuing her master's degree in trauma-informed education. She leads by example, providing daily mindful moments and grounding practices to help her students develop the habits of present-moment awareness for optimal learning.

Kellie and Hannah are dedicated to teaching courageously and helping all children feel safe, connected, represented, valued, and seen. They both believe that "it takes a calm brain to calm a brain" and that purposeful investment in youth social-emotional learning is a good place to begin this work.

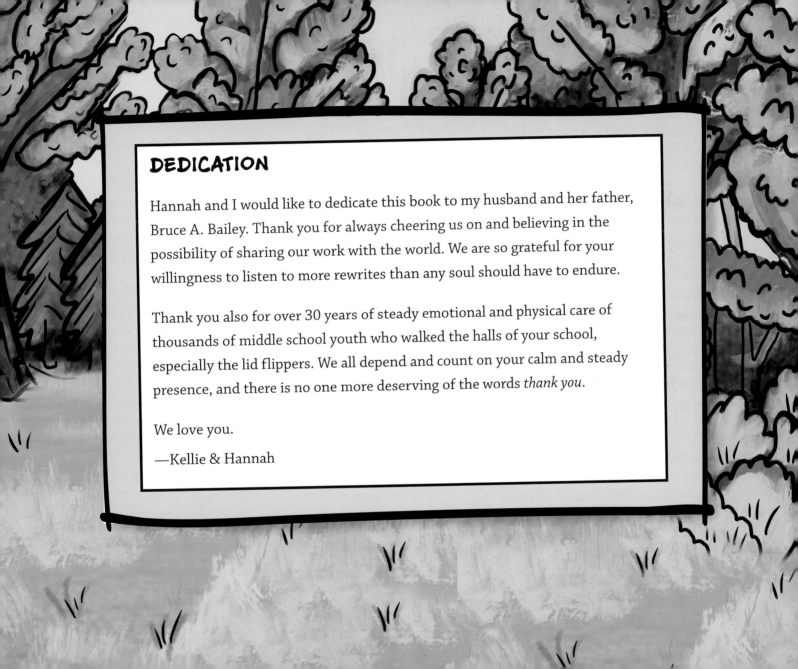

DEDICATION

Hannah and I would like to dedicate this book to my husband and her father, Bruce A. Bailey. Thank you for always cheering us on and believing in the possibility of sharing our work with the world. We are so grateful for your willingness to listen to more rewrites than any soul should have to endure.

Thank you also for over 30 years of steady emotional and physical care of thousands of middle school youth who walked the halls of your school, especially the lid flippers. We all depend and count on your calm and steady presence, and there is no one more deserving of the words *thank you*.

We love you.

—Kellie & Hannah